YOUR NEW JOURNEY

Michael Cason

YOUR NEW JOURNEY

Published by Spines
ISBN:979-8-89383-794-0

YOUR NEW JOURNEY

MICHAEL CASON

CONTENTS

DEDICATION

I would like to dedicate this book to all

Those who have loved once and given

yourself and your heart completely to

another and "have"

Been hurt, misused, rejected, betrayed,

and never thought you could love again.

Untill.....

Words of Honor

I WOULD LIKE TO THANK AND HONOR MY MOTHER ESTHER, FOR ALWAYS BEING AN EXAMPLE OF GOD'S LOVE IN MY LIFE AND NEVER GIVING UP ON ME. FOR ALWAYS SUPPORTING ME WHEN I HAD NO ONE ELSE.

I WOULD LIKE TO THANK PASTORS BRANDON BURNHAM AND DANIEL MANNING FOR BEING THERE FOR ME IN THE LORD AND BEING AN EXAMPLE OF BROTHERHOOD

AND A VERY SPECIAL THANKS TO APOSTLE GENE AND PROPHET ZENNIE HALL FOR BEING SPIRITUAL PARENTS TO ME IN MY TIMES OF NEED.

I WOULD LIKE TO GIVE A SPECIAL THANKS TO PROPHET MYLES KILBY FOR BEING A BROTHER, A FRIEND, AND BEING AN EXAMPLE AS A SON OF GOD THAT THROUGH CHRIST ALL THINGS ARE POSSIBLE

A SPECIAL THANKS TO AUTHOR AND PASTOR
CHRIS RODRIGUEZ FOR PRAYING AND ENCOURAGING
ME TO WRITE THIS BOOK.

I WOULD LIKE ALSO TO GIVE A SPECIAL
THANKS TO ALL MY FAMILY FOR ALSO
BEING THERE AND SACRIFICING FOR ME
WITH LOVE IN MY TIMES OF NEED IN MY LIFE

CHAPTER 1
LET'S TALK ABOUT LOVE

There are many of us on this journey of

Life that misinterprets what love is.

Many of us have seen love as a great weakness.

But today, I am here to tell you that true and

Pure love is the greatest power of all.

That great love is still here today.Real love

will stand for the truth.Pure love will see

Beyond the hurt and circumstances and

"Will see the truth."

John 14:6 (KJV)

Jesus saith unto him, "I am the way, the truth,

And the life; no man cometh unto the Father but by me."

Love is not just a feeling or an emotion; it is

"Much more than that."

John 15:13 KJV

Greater love hath no man than this:

that a man lay down his life for his friends.

THE WHOLE BIBLE IS A LOVE STORY

Reference "Billy Graham."

"There is nothing I mean absolutely nothing

That you are going through that Jesus

Christ has not gone through. He knows

Your pains, your sadness, your weakness,

Your strengths, all of your hurts,he knows

everything about you.He loves you so

much that he laid his life down for you.

One day, we were doing street ministry

And there was a homeless man being

Questioned by a police officer ,as though he

Had committed a crime . As I was walking

Towards them, The police officer just looked

At me coming towards them and walked

Away. As though all judgment has been

Released from his life.

I stepped up to the homeless man.

 began speaking to him. I told him,

I love you, and Jesus loves you to.

The man broke down in tears and he wrapped

His arms around me with tears streaming

Down his face; he said.....

NO ONE HAS EVER TOLD ME ME THAT BEFORE

I was shocked! The man was probably in his 50's.

I thought no one has ever told him they

Loved him before.If you look at this

Testimony. This is actually the Gospel of

JESUS CHRIST being illustrated to us.

That this man representing all of us

Had a judgment which we could not get free

From.Until Love came to set us free from

All penalty and judgment.

This is exactly what JESUS CHRIST did for us.

That penalty, that price we could not pay.

JESUS took up his life on the cross to

Redeem Gods children back to him.

And According to.....

JOHN 10:18 KJV

No man taketh it from me but I lay it

Down and I have power to take it again

This commandment have I received of my father

Jesus had the authority from God

On the earth to overthrow any

Decisions from man or from the

kingdom of darkness.But there was

a great power that Jesus functioned in.

The power thereof is love.There was

A prize, a reward for JESUS CHRIST

When he laid down his life. It was us. God

The father loved us so much he sent Jesus to

Pay the price we could not pay.

The love of the Father did something

We could not do.

John 3:16

For God so loved the world, that

he gave his only begotten son,

that whosoever believeth in him should

not perish, but have everlasting life

I would like now to share with you how this

Love came to me.One day I stumbled upon

A Christian recovery group. Let me explain.

I was driving around the island one day and

This desire came to me,I just thought I don't

Want to live this way anymore, I was tired of

The vicious cycle of addictions. Tired of all

 the depression, the loss of hope. The sense

 of having no purpose in my life.I drove up

On this property where I seen cars parked.

I just sat in my car for a few minutes and

I was just about to drive away until I seen a

Guy come out of the building. So I thought,

Well now I have to go over there.I walked

Up to the man and he said, are you here

To celebrate recovery? I said I guess so.

He had a name tag on that said Daniel

which was very significant to me.

So I took it as a sign from God that I was in

The right place. So he said come on in.

I went in and seen a group of people in a

Room singing songs to JESUS. I thought

Great, this is a church. I'm definitely not

Not going in there. So as I walked in there

I began to sing the words on the screen

And went back every week.

As I was going there, I also met the new

Pastors Brandon and Daniel. I met Pastor

Daniel at one of the recovery meetings

One night and asked him if he was there

for help also. He said no Actually I'm one

of the new Pastors here.A Different Daniel

I met a week prior. He then asked Me if I knew

Jesus and had a relationship with him?

I said, "no." To be honest I don't understand

The God and JESUS thing. He then told me

The simple words of the Gospel. Look, none

Of us would have never been good enough

For God. We all have fell short of His glory.

That's why he sent JESUS. With JESUS we

Are Good enough for God. Two weeks later

Something happened.

I had a bad relapse in my addictions.Now

it was around 5 a.m. and I haven't slept In

days.I was lying on the couch and I just

Broke down in tears and began crying out.

God,I hate my life. Please just kill me.I don't

Want to live anymore.Then all of a sudden I

Began to feel this peace come all over me. I

said what is this peace.I never felt this before.

Then I said the few words that changed my

My life forever. I SAID...

JESUS I ACCEPT YOU!!!

I can't describe the feeling other than it was

Like I breathed my first breath. I had this new

Life inside of me. I then told Pastor Brandon

What happened and he congratulationed

Me and said I had been born again.

I got saved. He then had me share my

Testimony with the church and my New

Journey had just begun. My days as a slave

Was over.Those chains of addictions are

forever broken off my life all thanks to the

Obedience and the blood of JESUS

CHRIST!

Let today be your day. Say this with me...

JESUS I ACCEPT YOU IN MY HEART TODAY. THANK YOU FOR SAVING ME. I BELIEVE THIS NEW LIFE I HAVE RECEIVED IS FOR THE FORGIVENESS OF ALL MY SINS AND BECAUSE YOU LIVE I LIVE ALSO. JESUS TEACH ME YOUR WAYS.JESUS I MAKE YOU THE LORD OF MY LIFE!

CHAPTER 2
YOUR FREE GIFT

If you have chosen to confess the Lord as

Your Savior, and receive him into your

Hearts, I would like to say congratulations!

You have now been transformed into a

Child of God. You have received a new

Identity.

"You have been pulled out of the kingdom

Of darkness into the kingdom of light.

The darkness in the Earth is sin.

We are not in darkness, but in the light.

Matthew 5:14-16 (KJV)

Ye are the light of the world. A city that is set on an hill cannot be hid. Neither do men light a candle, and put it under a bushel, but on a candlestick; and it giveth light unto all that are in the house. Let your light so shine before men, that they may see your good works and glorify your Father which is in heaven.

All things have been given to him and all

Authority belongs to JESUS. As our

Inheritance we have obtained and received

Every spiritual blessing

Ephesians1:3-5 KJV

3 Blessed be the God and father Jesus Christ

Who hath blessed us with all spiritual blessings

In heavenly places in heavenly places In Christ.

 4 According as he hath chosen us in him before

the foundation of the world that we should be

 holy and without blame before him in love.

5 having predestined us unto the adoption of

 children by Jesus Christ to himself According to

the good pleasure of his will.

See we were once orphans. We were once

Fatherless because of this reason.

Romans 8:9

But you are not in the flesh,but in

the spirit, if so be that the spirit

Of God dwell in you now, if any man have

Not the spirit of Christ; he is none of his

You are now his. You have his spirit.

When you asked Christ into your Hearts,

Confessed him lord and savior. You have

Have received the free gift of the Holy Spirt.

Ephesians 1 13-14

13 in whom ye also trusted, after that ye heard the word

Of truth, the Gospel of your salvation; in whom also after

That ye believed, ye were sealed with that holy spirit of promise

14 which is the earnest of our Inheritance until

the redemption of the purchased possession unto the

The praise of his glory

EPHESIANS 2:8-10

8 For by grace are ye saved through faith; and that not of

Yourselves; it is the gift of God: 9 not of works, lest any man

Should boast : 10 For we are his workmanship, created in

Christ Jesus unto good works, which God hath

before ordained that we should walk in them

We are not saved by our works but God

Created us in Christ to do good works.

We could have never pleased God with any

Thing we ever did.Jesus was the only thing

That pleased him.Our relationship with God

Was damaged. So he sent Jesus to restore

Our relationship. Jesus already paid the

Price for salvation, the forgiveness of our

Sins, and so he sits there with his hand

Extended for anyone that will receive him.

So now we have the Holy Spirit, our helper. The

Holy Spirit will teach us and always point us to

Jesus. So Jesus did not give us this free gift of

Salvation for us to continue in the things of the

world or in sin.Just as he gave all of himself for

us. He wants a mutual relationship where we

Are willing to give ourselves to him. Now he has

Given us something that will help sustain us.

Grace

His Grace is like a super power that when

He ask us to do something he will give us

This super power called GRACE.To equip

And empower us to get through anything

He has asked of us. We are still in the world

Of sin and darkness But we are no longer

Of this world. We are children of the light.

1st John 2 15-17

15 Love not the world neither the things that are in the world

If any man love the world, The love of the father is not in him

16 For all that is in the world, the lust of the flesh, the lust

Of the eyes, and the pride of life, is not of

the Father, but Is of the world.

17 And the world passeth away, and the lust thereof, but

He that doeth the will of God abideth for ever.

God has called us out of darkness which is

Sin. Not to continue in it, but to be free from

It. To walk in the fullness of God and

Everything he has given us. God has given

All of us a destiny and wants us to fulfill

It here on the earth.You may ask,what Is my

Purpose, what is my destiny? Well,our lives

Are hidden in Christ.

Colossians3:3

For ye are dead, and your life is

Hid with Christ in God

As you walk with Christ and follow him.

He will reveal your destiny to you as he

pleases.

YOU ARE NOW BORN AGAIN!

JOHN 3:3

Jesus answered and said unto him,

"Verily, verily, I say unto thee, except a

Man be born again, he cannot see the

Kingdom of God

Beloved you are now in the kingdom of God

Don't worry you have all the help you need,

The Holy Spirit in you will always help you!

1st Corinthians 2:12 KJV

12 Now we have received, not the spirit of the world, but the Spirit which is of God, that we might know the things that are freely given to us of God but the Spirit which is of God, that we might know the things that are freely given to us of God.

Jesus shows us what a true leader is.

We are called now to walk with him and

Follow him as he leads. What a true King

He is. He came not to be served, but to serve.

Mark 10:45

45 For even the Son of man came not to be ministered unto,

But to minister, and to give his life a ransom for many.

Jesus pioneered a way for us to live a

Selfless life and A life of Love, Abundance,

and to have Compassion for others.

CHAPTER 3
SOME VISIONS FOR YOU

The journey of the heart is the most

Amazing Journey you will have ever

Experienced.The Lord reveals to heal.

Matthew 22 37- 39

37 Jesus said to him, You shall love the lord your God

With all your heart, with all your soul, and with all your mind

38 This is the first and great commandment

39 And the second is like it; You shall Love your neighbor

As yourself

Here is an example of our heart 100% full

Of the Love of God, our Father.

OUR BEST WEAPON IS OUR HEART

FULLY SURRENDERED TO JESUS

MATTHEW 6;21.

FOR WHERE YOUR.

TREASURE IS.

THERE WILL.

YOUR HEART

BE ALSO.

PHILIPPIANS 4;7

AND THE PEACE OF GOD

WHICH PASSETH ALL

UNDERSTANDING SHALL

KEEP YOUR HEARTS AND

MINDS THROUGH CHRIST JESUS

MATTHEW 5;8

BLESSED ARE THE PURE.

IN HEART FOR THEY

SHALL SEE GOD.

PROVERBS 4;23

KEEP YOUR HEART WITH ALL

DILIGENCE FOR OUT OF IT ARE

THE ISSUES OF LIFE

When the enemy knows an area of our

Hearts that is not surrendered to the lord,he

Will try to use that to lure you further away

from the lord and from your purpose in him.

God wants us to have that relationship with him

That he so longed desired. God is a Jealous God.

He wants every area of our hearts.

*Idols can be anything we place above the Lord in our hearts.

IDOLS.

MONEY RELATIONSHIPS

CAREERS POSITIONS

PSALM 147;3

HE HEALETH THE BROKEN IN HEART

 AND BINDETH UP THEIR WOUNDS

PSALM 37;4

4 Delight thyself also in the Lord; and he shall give thee

The desires of thine heart.

When we delight in the Lord, He fills us with

The desires of our heart. His desires now

Become our desires. It's not that he doesn't

Want us to have these things. He does not

Want these things to have us. We are not to

Be slaves to anything. We belong to Jesus.

These material things are called resources.

God wants to use these resources to build

And expand his kingdom on the earth. For

God wishes no one perish,but all be saved.

There are times God will bless us with things just

out of his goodness.God is a giver.If every

area of our hearts are surrendered to

Jesus we can not be bought or lured away.

So we must ask ourselves. Is there anything

In my heart that is in the place where the

The Lord belongs.This next illustration

Will show some of the most common

We all have dealt with. Please give yourselves patience

As well. The healing of out hearts can

Be a process. So if your not seeing instant results

thats ok. Trust the lord's process.

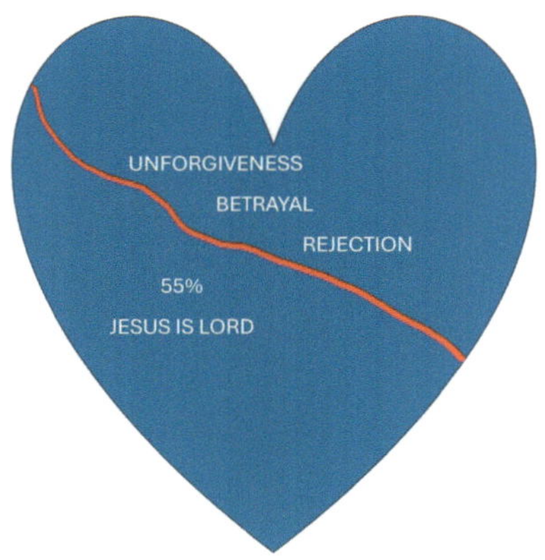

Let's talk about it. Rejection, many of us

Have experienced this. Whether it's in our

Marriages, friendships, school, even our

Workplace. Maybe you were hoping for

Something and you got the BIG NO.

Maybe you were in a friendship and your

Best friend took another's side against you.

You felt rejected, even betrayed.

Well don't worry, because healing is your

Portion, and just acknowledging the pain in

Your heart is a big part of the battle.Victory

is assured. Rejection can be a tough one. Lets face it.

Most of us all want to be accepted.

Let's look to the one that faced

The highest level of persecution which is rejection.

The very people Jesus was giving his life

for was mocking him, physically and verbally abusing

him.To the point where he was unrecognizable.

But what did he say. He said father

forgive them for they do not know what

They are doing. We must take that into consideration.

That most of the time people do

not know what they are doing when

they are doing things we perceived as hateful.

When we carry around that rejection

It can prevent us from moving foward

Into the things God has for us

because we might not move in the direction

hes told us to go because of fear of

being rejected. So let go of that fear,

Let go of that rejection Today.

You are loved, you have been

forgiving.You are accepted by God.

Your identity comes from God and he

approves you and your destiny.

You are created in his image and

You are his child. Lets show

 the same grace and mercy we have

received from our father to others.

Betrayal, now this one can be

Really nasty. Most Commonly,

Betrayal happens in families,or

those we hold close to our

hearts.Betrayal also happens

Alot in the feild of Buisness.

 I have been revealed this simple

truth that has set me free.

Most betrayal happens because

of this one thing.The LOVE OF MONEY.

The Love of money is the root of

All evil. Reference 1st Timothy 6:10

This is one of the reasons for

Keeping a pure heart and pure

motives because we do not want

the love of money to have our

Heart. Now we all have been

Betrayed at one point but let's not

Allow that from keeping us

moving foward.

Romans 12:21

21 be not overcome of evil,but

Overcome evil with good.

Now let us shine the light on

the next one Unforgiveness. We all have

Experienced this one. Someone hurt us,

Offended us.Did something to us where

We hold a grudge against the person.

Maybe it plays over and over in your mind.

We must forgive and we must do it quickly.

We must regain the territory back in our

Hearts.

Matthew 18 21-22

21 then came peter to him and said, lord, how oft shall my

Brother sin against me and I forgive him? Till seven times?

22 Jesus saith unto him, I say not unto thee, until seven times:

but until seventy times seven

Let's do the math.70 x 7= 490 times we

Must forgive someone who has sinned

against us.

We might have to forgive the person more

Than once before we have actually forgiven

Them. Love holds no record of wrongs.

To forgive is to forget about it. When we

Choose not to do so we are actually

Saying here enemy have my heart. If there

Was an injustice done.Give it over to Jesus.

We must forgive others as we have been forgiving.

Romans 12;19

Dearly beloved,avenge not yourselves,

But rather give place unto wrath, for it is written

vengeance is Mine; I will repay, saith the Lord

When we Choose to

Love others there Is a chance

someone may not receive you

Or you could get hurt. That's why

Forgiveness is so important.

You are choosing life and

protecting your heart from any

darkness entering in.

We are going to forgive and give the lord

These areas back in our hearts. Do you

Agree? This next illustration is just a few

Scriptures to affirm our healed hearts

And giving those areas back to who they

Belong to .OUR LORD JESUS CHRIST.

So that we can receive the fullness of what

God has for us. Now this is

Something we grow and mature

In. Did you perfectly ride a bike

The first time you got on.

Im sure everyone said no.

This is something that becomes

a very important part of our walk

With Jesus Christ.

1st John 4:8

HE THAT LOVETH NOT,

KNOWETH NOT GOD.

FOR GOD IS LOVE.

GALATIANS 6:9

AND LET US NOT BE

WEARY IN WELL

DOING, FOR IN DUE SEASON

WE SHALL REAP IF WE FAINT NOT

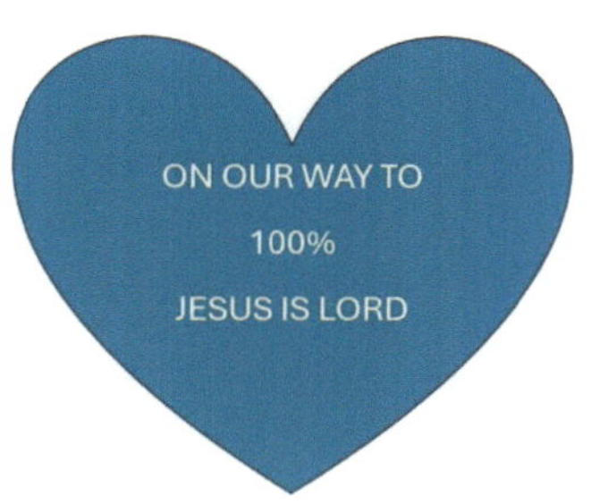

1ST John 4:7

BELOVED, LET US LOVE ONE

ANOTHER, FOR LOVE IS OF GOD

AND EVERYONE THAT LOVETH IS BORN OF GOD

AND KNOWETH GOD FOR GOD IS LOVE

The hidden motives in our hearts are

just as important as the actions we take.

Now lets take communion with the Lord

Go ahead and get a piece of bread and

Some kind of liquid, juice or water will work.

Psalm 26:2

Examine me, o lord,

And prove me; try my

Reins and my heart

1stCorinthians11;28

But let a man examine himself

and so let him eat of that bread

and drink of that cup

So take your time here and examine your

Heart. Repent of anything you need to.The

lord himself will reveal these things.

*Repent- to change your mind.

So the holy spirit may give you your own

Words to say. But here is a prayer you can say

Lord I hold onto nothing in my heart

That does not belong. All bitterness, all

Unforgiveness, all hate, or any darkness

In my heart. Lord Jesus, I release these

Things to you. Lord shine your light so

Bright upon my heart, my soul, and my

Body. If There is anything there that does

not belong I ask that you remove

it now IN JESUS NAME

You may eat the bread as you feel the

Peace to do so, lord we partake of your body.

JESUS my body is your body

Lord we thank you for your precious Blood,

And lord we thank you for the power that's

In Your blood, and lord we accept the new covenant of this blood, and we partake of it

Now and the power thereof. Now drink.

Thank you JESUS. JESUS IS LORD

Make this an everyday thing between you and the lord. keeping our hearts pure before the Lord.

CHAPTER 4
THE FOUNDATION OF LOVE

The first thing we must understand about

Love is. That love is not from this earth

But it is from above. God is love and love is

From God. Love was sent here in the flesh

By the spirit of God and love manifested

Himself as Jesus Christ. God in the flesh.

So,if love is not from this earth,but it is from

God.That makes it a great foundation.

It can never be destroyed.The world

We live in needs this love that was sent.

Now we, as the children of God get to carry

His light and his love. Love is effective and

People respond to love. So lets stay in LOVE

Lets look at this illustration and love

Scriptures to help us remain on the

FOUNDATION OF LOVE

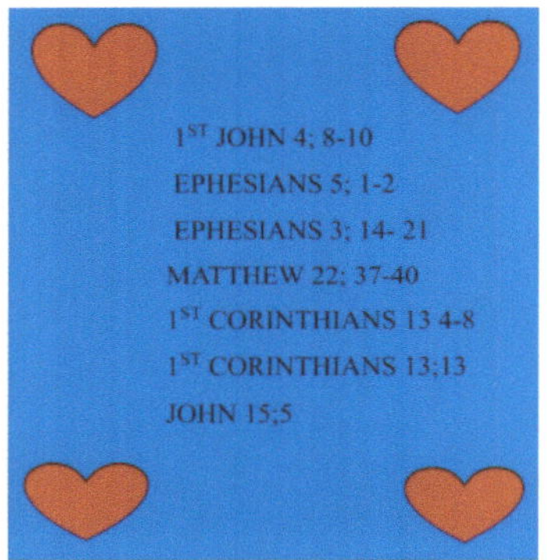

1st John 4;8-10

8 He that loveth not knoweth not God, for God is love

9 In this was manifested the love of God towards us,

Because that God sent his only begotten Son into

The world, that we might live through him.

10 Herein is love, not that we loved God, but that he

Loved us, and sent his son to be the propitation for

Our sins.

Below I will put a simple explanation and the holy spirit will
teach you as well

1ST JOHN 4;8 love is from him so if you DON'T LOVE YOU CAN'T SAY YOU KNOW GOD

1ST John 4;9 JESUS WAS GOD'S MANIFESTED LOVE

1ST JOHN 4;10 GOD LOVED US FIRST

Ephesians 5; 1-2

1 Be ye therefore followers of God, as dear children

2 and walk in love as Christ also Hath loved us, and hath

Given himself for us an offering and a sacrifice to God

For a sweet smelling savour.

Ephesians 5; 1

We are to follow god as his children not as

Strangers or orphans. We are his children.

Ephesians 5; 2

Here is telling us to walk in love just as He Did. When Jesus walked in love he was carrying the cross. We can walk in that same power which is the love of the father in us.

APOSTLE PAUL'S PRAYER

EPHESIANS 3;14-21

14 For this cause I bow my knees unto the father of our

Lord Jesus Christ

15 of whom the whole family in heaven and earth is named

16 That he would grant you, according to the riches of his glory, to be strengthened with might by his spirit in the inner man

17 That Christ may dwell in your hearts by faith, that ye,

Being rooted and grounded in love

18 may be able to comprehend with all the saints what is

The breadth, and length, and depth, and height

19 And to know the love of Christ, which passeth knowledge, that ye might be filled with all the fullness of God.

20 now unto him that is able to do exceeding abundantly

Above all that we ask or think, according to the power that worketh in us

21 unto him be Glory in the church by Christ Jesus throughout all ages, world without end amen

The context of Paul's prayer here is love.

Lets remember the man that prayed this

Prayer used to be called Saul and Saul

Used to murder Christians. Until Love came

And confronted him. JESUS taking him

Captive and making him a slave of

Righteousness.I believe this Revelation

Of Ephesians 3;20. A man that murdered

God's people. LOVE captured him, forgave

Him and gave him a new life. That love is

Available to all of us.Exceeding and

Abundantly all we can ask or think.

Matthew 22; 37-40

37 Jesus said unto him, thou shalt love the lord thy God

With all thy heart, and with all thy soul, and with all thy mind

38 This is the first and great commandment.

39 And the second is like unto it, Thou shalt love thy neighbor as thyself

40 On these two commandments hang all the law and the prophets

Lets keep it simple here;Love God with

Every part of yourself and love others as

you love yourself.

CHARITY IS LOVE IN ACTION

1ST CORINTHIANS 13;4-8

4 Charity suffereth long, and is kind, charity envieth not;

Charity vaunteth not itself, is not puffed up

5 Doth not behave itself unseemly; seeketh not her own, is not easily provoked, thinketh no evil

6 Rejoiceth not in iniquity, but rejoices in the truth

7 Beareth all things, believeth all things, hopeth all things

Endureth all things

*This is describing what walking in love is. Love in action.

When we walk in love we are walking in Gods power to

Endure all things in the earth.

1st Corinthians 13; 13

And now abideth faith, hope, charity, these

three, but the greatest of these is charity.

Faith worketh by love. Reference Galatians 5;6

HEBREWS 11;1

Now faith is the substance of things hoped for,

the evidence of things not seen.

Without love we are nothing.Reference 1st Corinthians 13;2

JAMES 2;18

Yea,a man may say,Thou hast faith,and I have works,

shew me thy faith without thy works and I will shew

thee my faith by my works.

WORDS OF JESUS STAY CONNECTED

JOHN 15;5

I am the vine, ye are the branches; he that abideth in me,

And I in him, The same bringeth forth much fruit; for

Without me ye can do nothing

Can anything grow without being rooted,

Connected to its life source. Well us as dear

Children of God must be connected to our

Life source as well.Which is Jesus. The way

The truth and The life.

The holy spirit will always help us stay

Connected and in fellowship with Jesus!

John 15;9

As the father hath loved me, so have I

Loved you; continue ye in my love

We never would have known what the love

Of the father is, if he did not send the son.

Just as he sent Jesus, he may send you

To as one of the Disciples of LOVE.

STAY CONNECTED,STAY ROOTED,

STAY GROUNDED IN THE FOUNDATION OF LOVE

CHAPTER 5
YOU BELONG

Beloved, You belong to God the father.

And to the head which is Christ and to

His glorious body which is the church.

One time in our lives we have all

Experienced where we felt like maybe

We didn't fit in, or we didn't belong.

Well the truth is. Until we accepted Jesus,

We didn't.We were all born to be born again

And born again to be free from sin.

We must know who we are, where we are

Positioned and who we belong to.

2 Corinthians 5:17-18 (KJV)

17 Therefore, if any man be in Christ,

 he is a new creature: old things are passed

away; behold, all things are become new.

18 And all things are of God, who hath reconciled

us to himself by Jesus Christ, and hath given to

us the ministry of reconciliation;

When Jesus walked the earth he spent

Time with his family, his chosen Apostles,

The afflicted, the lost and the ashamed.

But most of all he spent time the most

With his father.Jesus brought this

Incredible revelation to us that we are no

Longer orphans but we are now through his

Redemptive blood. Children of God.

Think about it. The one who created it all

Calls us his children.

Romans 8;15-17

15 For ye have not received the spirit of bondage

again to fear; but ye have received the spirit of

adoption whereby We cry ABBA Father.

16 The spirit itself beareth witness with our spirit that

We are the children of God

17 and if children, then heirs of God, and joint heirs with

Christ; if so be that we suffer with him, that we

May also be glorified together.

We are not only his children but we have

Received an inheritance.

Ephesians 1;3-4

3 blessed be the God and Father of our

Lord Jesus Christ, who hath blessed us with

 all spiritual blessings in heavenly places In Christ

4 according as he hath chosen us in him before the

Foundation of the world, that we should be holy

And without blame before him in love

Say these out loud.

I am a child of God

I have received an inheritance

I am chosen by my father

1st Corinthians 6;20

20 for ye are bought with a price; therefore glorify God

In your body and in your Spirit which are Gods

You have been purchased by the obedience

And the blood of Jesus Christ.You have

Received a promise and you are sealed

With that promise.

Ephesians 1;13

13 In whom ye also trusted, after that ye heard the word of

Truth, the gospel of your salvation, in whom also after that

Ye believed ye were sealed with that holy spirit of promise

He will never leave you nor forsake you and

He will teach you great and mighty things.

John 2;27

but the anointing which ye have received of him abideth

in you and ye need not that any man teacheth you of all

things, and is truth, and is no lie , and even as it hath

 taught you, ye shall abide in him.

The Holy Spirit is our best teacher,but

Remember being the body of Christ. The

Holy Spirit may teach through you and others

The Holy Spirit will work through us to build

And edify the body of Christ. So we may

Grow into the fullness of God. As we are

Growing in Christ we will begin to

Lead people to Jesus.We need Jesus and

each other to support and function

Together.We are positioned in Christ and

We belong to him.Jesus is our good Shepherd

John 10; 27- 28

27 My sheep hear my voice, and I know them ,

and they Follow me 28 And I give unto them eternal

 Life; and they shall never perish; neither shall any man

 pluck them out of my hand

2 Timothy 2 ;13

13 If we are faithless, He remains faithful,

for he cannot deny himself.

Through the lord's faithfulness in my

Personal life. He has taught me so much.

Some of the greatest things he's taught me

Is selflessness, how to serve others, loyalty,

Enduring with him in the hard times.

And the most important thing.What love is.

There is such an importance of learning

These things.We are apart of him and apart

Of the body of Christ.We must not allow

The things and cares of the world to divide

Us from each other.We must avoid foolish

Things such as being in competition with

One another.Those things can divide us

If we allow it to happen.But we will not.

Matthew 12;25

25 And Jesus knew their thoughts, and said unto them

Every kingdom divided against itself is brought to desolation

And every city or house divided against itself shall not stand

That is the truth. I also tell you today that

Even as a house divided cant stand. A body

Divided cannot function.The Father, the

Son, And the Holy Spirit has taught us the

Importance of unity of the faith.

Beloved, always remember to stay, walk,

And stand on the foundation of Love.

Stay connected to Jesus, he is our vine

Our life source.Try hard to stay in unity

With the family of God. Don't allow

The enemy to have any area in your heart.

I pray that the Lord keeps you and continues

To prosper you.

You are never alone. Beloved, you are loved.

John13:34-35

34 "A new commandment I give unto you: that ye

 love one another as I have loved you,

that ye also love one another."

35"By this shall all men know

that ye are my disciples."

If ye have love one to another.

John14:15

If ye love me, keep my commandments

I want to say "thank you" to all who have

Read this book. I hope this has blessed you.

"I love you. God loves you, and JESUS IS LORD."

Afterword

We would love to hear from you, if you would like to Submit a testimony please do. You can contact us at

Michaelcasonministries@gmail.com

www.ingramcontent.com/pod-product-compliance
Lightning Source LLC
Chambersburg PA
CBHW040506160726
48005CB00038B/103